W9-AYA-724

No Ordinary Fish

WRITTEN BY ANNE LAWRENCE

MODERN CURRICULUM PRESS

PROJECT DIRECTOR: Susan Cornell Poskanzer
ART DIRECTOR: Lisa Olsson

MODERN CURRICULUM PRESS
13900 Prospect Road, Cleveland, Ohio 44136
Simon & Schuster • A Paramount Communications Company

Copyright © 1993 by McClanahan Book Company, Inc. All rights reserved.

This edition is published simultaneously in Canada by
Globe/Modern Curriculum Press, Toronto.

PHOTOGRAPHY CREDITS
Front Jacket: © Marty Snyderman
© Gary Bell/The Wildlife Collection p. 9; © G. I. Bernard/Animals Animals p. 8 inset;
© W. Gregory Brown/Animals Animals pp. 6, 7;
© Dave Fleetham/Tom Stack & Associates pp. 1, 2, 3, 12, 13; © Howard Hall pp. 14, 15;
© Richard Herrmann/The Wildlife Collection pp.10, 11; © Chris Huss/The Wildlife Collection p. 8;
© Brian Parker/Tom Stack & Associates p. 7 inset; © James D. Watt pp. 4, 5;
© F. Stuart Westmorland/Tom Stack & Associates p. 16

ISBN 0-8136-1144-X (STY PK) ISBN 0-8136-1145-8 (BB) ISBN 0-8136-1146-6 (SB)

10 9 8 98

SANDBAR SHARK

I'm a shark, and I'm no ordinary fish.

I have a big brain, a great sense of smell, and excellent eyesight. All of these things help make me one of the most powerful fish in the sea.

The Shark Is

WHALE SHARK

NO ORDINARY FISH!

Caribbean Reef Shark

The Shark Is No

I breathe through gills, like other fish. But I'm not like any other fish. My skin has tiny, hard-as-teeth scales. My skeleton is lighter, too, so I travel farther and faster! I cut through the water like a sharp knife.

SHARK GILLS

ORDINARY FISH!

Sand Tiger Shark

Mako Shark Teeth

The Shark Is No

Many of us have rows and rows of sharp teeth. We have grinding teeth, cutting teeth, ripping teeth, and crushing teeth. Our teeth never stop growing. When they wear out, more grow in. Some teeth are pointed backward, so dinner does not escape. Other fish don't have teeth like these!

NURSE SHARK

ORDINARY FISH!

Blue Shark

The Shark Is

My favorite food is fresh fish. I see and smell it from far away. I hear it too... right through my skin. If a tasty fish swims near me, I feel its heart beat through my skin. I see it with my eyes. I smell it with my nose.

No Ordinary Fish!

People tell horrible stories about us. Really, most sharks never bother people. But it is smart not to forget a few important rules when you're at the ocean.

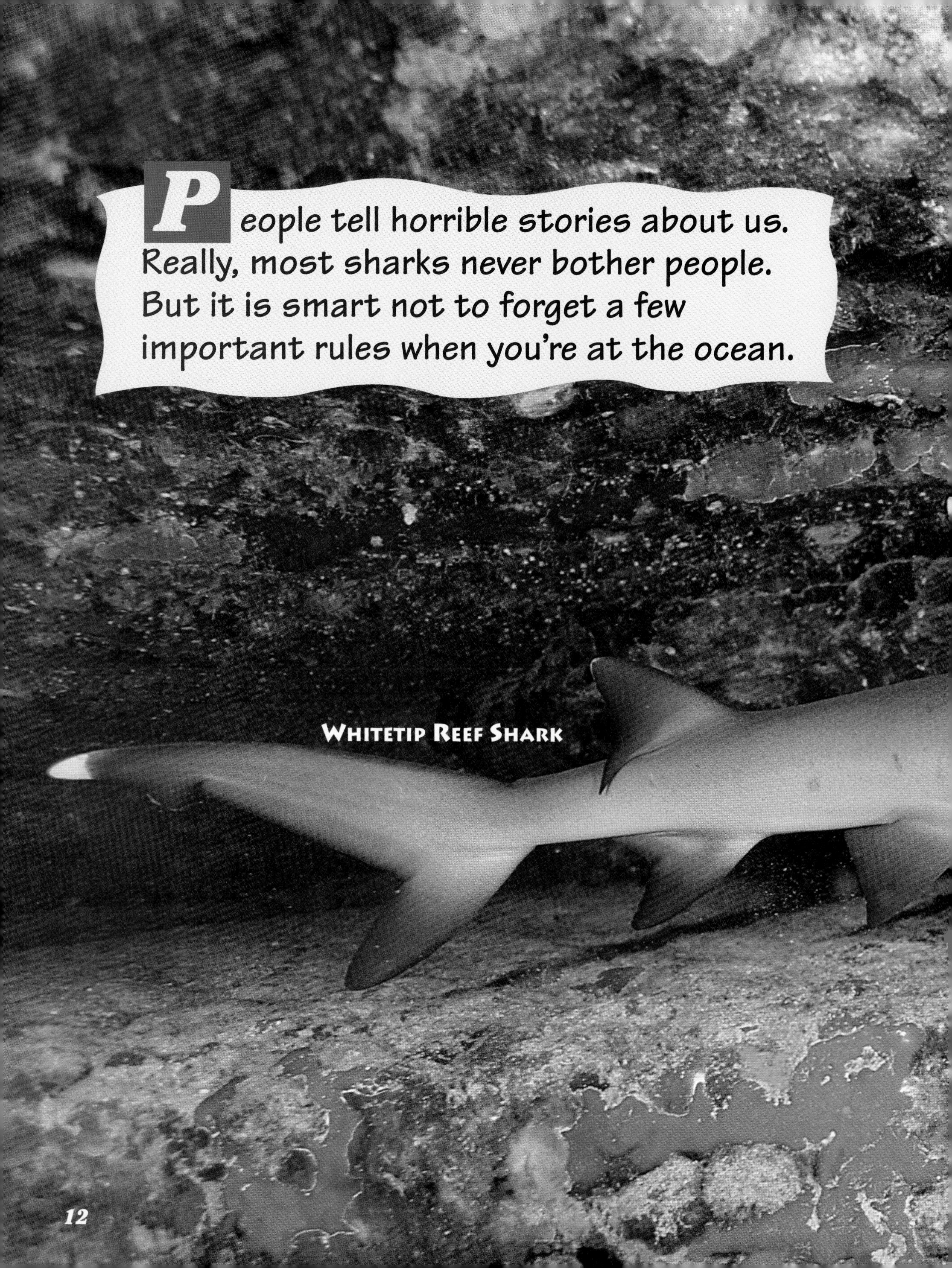

WHITETIP REEF SHARK

Shark Warnings!

1. Never swim or dive alone.
2. Never swim at night or in dirty water where it is hard to spot a shark.
3. Leave the water if you see a shark.

Sharks have been swimming in the seas since dinosaurs walked on the earth – more than 450 million years. I don't have many enemies. I swim faster than almost everyone else – and I'm smart.

So I will probably be around for a good, long time.

Great White Shark

Baby Horn Shark

Basking Shark

ZEBRA SHARK
HAMMERHEAD SHARK

SHARK FACTS

▼ There are over 300 different kinds of sharks.

▼ Some sharks are 60 feet long. Others are only a few inches long.

▼ A shark's teeth don't stay put. New teeth come in at the back and move forward. Because the teeth move, many fall out.

▼ Whale sharks are enormous, like some whales. But they eat only small fish and plankton. Plankton are tiny, floating plants and animals.

▼ Great White sharks may be the most dangerous sharks. They eat large fish and other animals like sea lions.

▼ Hammerhead sharks are strange-looking creatures with eyes that may be more than three feet apart.

Silky Sharks